BLUEBIRDS

David W. Frasure

Copple House Books, *Publisher*
Road's End
Lakemont, Georgia 30552

For information about *Bluebirds*, the author of *Bluebirds*
or *Bluebirds Music* write the publisher.

Illustrations by Thomas Severa

First Printing 1978
Second Printing 1979
Third Printing 1980

Printed for the publisher by
CHB Printing & Binding, Lakemont Georgia 30552

To Allison

Chapter 1

Emerging from the rear corner of the small bus station, Kris walked along side the building toward the front. As he walked the vibration from his footsteps on the pavement felt strange to his legs, a sensation he had not experienced in so many years that it would give a young schoolboy a challenge to count them. Stopping at the sidewalk, he looked up and down the main street of the small, northern Illinois town, then leaned up against the dirty, brick front of the bus station.

It was the end of May and the sun shown brightly in the clear afternoon sky. As he waited for the bus to arrive small beads of perspiration formed across his forehead, the renewal of another sensation that had not been experienced in a long while. All of his inner senses reacquainted themselves with his physical body, with life, and with living.

Canvassing the street with his eyes Kris saw her parents waiting in the car parked on the street just a short distance beyond the bus loading zone. Eleanor Haynes sat behind the steering wheel fanning herself with a newspaper, Fred sitting motionless on the opposite side of the car wearing his straw fishing hat, the window rolled down, his arm resting on the door.

Minutes passed quickly as Kris continued to familiarize himself with the sounds from the small town: laughing and yelling of children in the park across the way, cars moving up and down the street, the sound of a distant airplane flying overhead, and murmured words from conversations of passing people.

As the bus turned the corner and headed up the street towards the bus station, Kris changed from his relaxed position up against the building and stood straight as he waited for it to stop. Air brakes hissing, the bus came to a gentle stop, doors opening. His heart began to beat rapidly, almost a flutter, as the anticipation grew within him. Taking one step backwards he leaned against the side of the building as the people began to unload. Finally, she stepped from the bus, looking in all directions for her parents.

Kris savored the joy as his physical eyes once again gazed upon this beautiful woman, one of God's most magnificent creations. Allison was twenty-two years old, stood five feet, eight inches tall, had short, brown hair, dark eyes, a face and figure that would make any artist drool, and skin more tender and soft than any newborn baby. She was returning home for the summer after completing her junior year at college.

Continuing to look around for her parents, she saw Kris leaning against the building. Her eyes locked with his and Kris looked through her eyes into her soul to a depth far greater than the distance that spans the universe. Time ceased as their souls once again reunited.

After several seconds Allison gave a weak, but tender smile to Kris, then turned and saw her parents approaching. She ran the few short steps to meet them, hugged, then talked as the attendant unloaded the baggage from the compartments in the side of the bus. Kris continued to watch Allison and her parents while his mind filled with memories of their times together, of their love, of the joy and happiness they once brought to each other, and of the joy that Allison was unknowingly bringing to him now.

Allison and her parents picked up the several suitcases and walked toward the car. Kris watched with a smile on his lips and a swelling in his heart as they drove away. He walked to the newsstand, bought a paper, tucked it under his arm, picked up his small, well-worn suitcase and began the walk to Allison's house.

The walk to Allison's home should have taken about fifteen minutes but Kris wandered around the town for several hours giving Allison and her family time to get settled after her return home.

Chapter 2

Kris stood on the sidewalk in front of the Haynes' home. It was an older, well kept, wood house, two stories and a porch with a wooden railing that spanned the entire width of the house. A large bench swing hung from the ceiling on the extreme right end of the porch. The lot was of average size and two large weeping willow trees, one on either side of the walk leading to the front step, almost hid the house from view.

Walking slowly up the front walk onto the porch, he knocked on the wooden screen door. Todd, Allison's fourteen year old brother, came to the door. Kris explained that he was answering the ad in the newspaper concerning a room for rent. Eleanor came to the door, stepped out onto the porch and extended her hand to Kris, "Hello, I'm Eleanor Haynes. Can I help you?"

"Yes. I'm Kris McDaniels. I'm answering your ad about a room for rent."

Eleanor looked at the freshly rolled paper under Kris' arm. "Doesn't even look like you've opened the paper to read it. I know you couldn't have seen it in another paper because today is the first time for the ad."

"You're very observant, Mrs. Haynes, but I saw the ad elsewhere."

"Well, the room is upstairs with its own private bath. I'll expect no loud noise or disturbances. If you want a TV or radio you'll have to provide your own, but you can share ours if you'd like. Did you want the room and board, or just the room?"

"I'll take the room and meals if that's okay. I'll take home cooking to a restaurant anytime, and you look like a good cook to me."

Eleanor gave a shy smile of thanks, then continued, "How long do you plan to be in town? And if I may ask, what will you be doing here?"

"I may be here through the end of August, and I'm just here to relax and make some new friends."

"I see. Is there a chance that you'll be staying longer than August?"

"No, I don't think so. I feel certain that I'll be gone by then."

They continued their discussion for several more minutes. When Eleanor was convinced that Kris was the right person to rent the room, she told him that it would be forty dollars each week in advance. Kris pulled a new wallet from his left rear pocket, the only contents of which was two new twenty dollar bills, removed them, and gave them to Eleanor. She looked at the wallet very curiously, then at his small suitcase. "Is that your only piece of luggage?"

"Yes, everything I need is in there," Kris replied assuredly.

Eleanor took Kris inside and introduced him to her husband, Fred. They spoke for a few minutes, then Eleanor called Allison from the kitchen.

As Allison walked into the front room her eyes once again met Kris' and she stopped abruptly in the middle of her steps. Kris smiled warmly as Allison stood looking him straight in the eyes. Eleanor introduced them and Allison spoke, "Yes, I remember you from the bus station a few hours ago. Glad to meet you."

Eleanor asked Todd to show Kris his room and around the house. As they headed up the stairs to Kris' room, Eleanor called out to them, "Supper will be ready in about thirty minutes."

It was dark, and Kris lay across the front porch swing enjoying the fragrance of the cool night air. The television played in the background with its sound drifting through the slightly opened windows.

Allison came out onto the front porch and Kris started to sit up. "Oh, no," Allison said, "stay there. I'll sit over here on the chair. You look too comfortable and relaxed to be disturbed." Kris smiled and returned to his position.

"Just lying here enjoying the smell of the night air," Kris said in a soft voice. "Can you smell the sweetness in the air? Do you know what it is?"

"I really hadn't paid that much attention." Allison took in a deep breath, then exhaled. "Yes . . . yes, I do smell it. What is it?"

"Those are blueberry bushes that have just finished budding and are now starting to grow berries. The berries are very tiny and green now, but in a month or six weeks they will be ready to pick." Kris paused for a moment, then concluded, "They're early this year."

Allison looked curious. "I've never heard of such a thing. I don't know of any blueberries around here."

Sniffing the air lightly a few more times, Kris explained, "Their fragrance carries for miles. The bushes are out in the country, over a mile from here. I remember when I once lived in the northern part of Minnesota as a kid. All year I would wait for the time when the blueberry bushes would bud just so I could smell them at night. I used to leave my bedroom window open and curl up under the covers trying to keep warm in the cold night air, just so I could smell the blueberry bushes. Such a simple thing, but it was something I always waited for, just like kids wait for Christmas nowadays. Don't think I'll ever forget that."

Inquiring, Allison asked, "Is that where you're from, Minnesota?"

"No, but I lived there once, a long, long time ago."

With a little sarcasm in her voice, Allison said, "You say that like you're an old man or something."

Looking at her out of the corner of his eye Kris just smiled, said nothing, closed his eyes once again and took another deep breath. From the front room he could hear Fred speak, "Well, I think I've had it for today. I'm going to bed." He heard Fred fold the newspaper and drop it to the floor, then give a short grunt as he lifted himself out of the chair. His footsteps led to the front door. The screen door opened and Fred peeked his head around the corner. "Goodnight, Allison. I'm going to bed. It's nice to have you back home again."

"It's good to be back, Daddy," Allison said, then finished, "see you in the morning."

Kris sat up in the swing, "Goodnight, Fred."

"Goodnight, Kris."

Fred closed the door and could be heard walking up the stairs to the second floor.

Looking at Allison, Kris spoke, "Will you do me a favor, Allison?"

Allison looked sort of puzzled. "Sure, if I can."

"Would you go upstairs and tell your dad goodnight, and tell him how you feel about him. And on your way, stop and drag Todd away from the TV for a few minutes and take him along with you."

Looking surprised, almost shocked, Allison said, "Well, yes, I guess I can. I guess I should have thought of that myself." She stood up and went into the house. Kris could hear Todd's objections as Allison pulled him from the floor and took him upstairs.

She returned in about five minutes and sat down next to Kris on the swing. "You're a strange man," she said, "do you know that?"

"Do you think so?" Kris answered with a smile.

"I know that I should have thought of going upstairs, especially just after returning home from school . . . but you surprised me by asking to do it. Why was it so important to you? Why did you want me to do it?"

Kris laid his head back on the swing, then turned his head to face Allison. "There's nothing wrong with telling someone you love them, and how you feel about them. Sometimes we feel these things, but we never say them. We always put it off until later. And sometimes, later just never comes. If we feel love toward someone we should tell them. That's not so bad, is it?"

"No. And I guess you're right about putting things off. I do that all the time."

Kris looked at the porch ceiling. "It usually only takes a minute and I think we feel better for it. And besides, we can never regret the fact that we didn't say it. I think it's very fulfilling to express our feelings to people we care about but we must take time to do it."

Looking down into her lap, and speaking slowly she replied, "I guess you're right." Allison paused, then asked, "If you don't like someone or if you hate someone . . . do you believe we should tell them that also?"

"No. I don't think so. Hate, I believe, is really misdirected love. Normally, when we love, we give it to another person or thing. Hate is when we love our own selfish selves so much, in such a limited way, that another's actions won't fit into our scheme of life. We get upset because of what we *think* they have done to us. So we wind up hating. It's really very simple. And I think one of the most beautiful things is that when we truly learn to love, we no longer have any capacity to hate."

With a somewhat confused look on her face, Allison said, "I think I understand what you said, but maybe not completely."

"That's okay. Remember I'm strange," Kris said jokingly. He looked back at the ceiling and gave the swing a litte push with his feet. They both swung quietly for a few minutes. With his eyes closed Kris quietly asked, "How long has your dad been sick?"

"How did you know that?"

"Oh, I just figured it out. I can tell by the way he moves that he has heart trouble and I know that your mother decided to rent the room to make additional money while your dad is out of work."

"You're pretty smart," Allison said, then added quietly, "for a strange man." They both laughed. She continued, "And what else do you know about our family?"

"Well, I know that you have an older sister that's

married, and that she has a little girl about nine or ten years old."

Allison gasped, "And how did you know that?"

"It was extremely difficult," Kris said with a twinge of wryness in his voice. "I saw their family picture on the fireplace mantel in the front room."

"And how did you know it was my sister in the picture? It could have been my brother and his wife."

"She looks too much like your mother and you. I'm not that easy to fool. I may be strange . . . but I'm not dumb," Kris said as a smile spread across his face.

Allison's voice grew quite serious and spoke scarcely above a whisper, "I don't know whether I've ever met anyone quite like you before, Kris. When I saw you at the bus station today I felt like I knew you, but yet I didn't. And your eyes . . . there's something about them . . . I can't describe it . . . it's almost like there's an inner power of some type speaking to me. Your eyes are black. I don't think I've ever seen black eyes before. They're as black as the hair on your head . . . your dark skin, your quiet manner, your soft voice . . . you're just different."

Allison paused for a moment, then continued, "Where are you from, Kris? Just in the few hours you've been here you seem to know a lot about this place, our town, and the places around here."

With some reluctance in his voice, Kris said, "Oh . . . I've been through here before."

"When was that?"

"Oh, not too long ago."

Allison moved around on the swing, and sat sideways facing Kris. "You seem to be avoiding my questions."

"No, not really. I just don't know how to answer them."

"You mean you don't know where you're from, or the last time you were here?"

With more reluctance and a slight hesitation in his voice, Kris answered, "Well, Allison . . . let's just say I've traveled around a lot."

"Okay . . . I'm sorry. You're right. It's none of my business."

"No, no, no." Kris said, "I'm not trying to cut you short. As we get to know each other a little more, I think you'll understand me better."

They swung quietly for a while longer, then Allison spoke. "Well, Christopher, I think I'll go to bed," as she started to get up. Kris reached over and put his hand on hers, stopping her. "My name isn't Christopher, it's Krisna. Kris is spelled with a K, you know K-R-I-S."

"Oh, I'm sorry. Krisna did you say? I've never heard that name before. How do you spell it?"

"K-R-I-S-N-A. It's a derivation of a name used in India. Krisna James McDaniels, that's me. And you . . . you're Allison Melissa Haynes, right?"

"And where did you see that around the house?" Allison said with a surprised look on her face and inflection in her voice.

"I didn't see it anyplace. There was no doubt about it. I just knew that your middle name had to be Melissa."

Chapter 3

Awakening at 4:45 in the morning, Kris got out of bed and went into his bathroom where he showered, shaved and brushed his teeth. As he finished dressing he took a deep breath, then opened his bedroom door a few inches. He stood inside the room leaning against the wall, looking through the small opening in the doorway which led into the hall, waiting for his day to begin.

A few minutes passed, then Eleanor opened their bedroom door and stepped into the hallway with a horrified look on her face. She stood there and brought her hands to her face as Kris stepped into the hall, walked over and hugged her. "He's gone," Eleanor said softly, almost in a whisper, "he's gone . . . my Fred . . . he's gone . . . he's dead."

Kris tucked her head against his chest and continued

to hold her gently. He looked into the bedroom and saw Fred in bed lying on his back. Over in the far corner Kris could see Fred's spirit hovering near the ceiling. Kris spoke to Fred with his heart and mind. As he did so, Fred's spirit moved to the hallway where it stayed near Eleanor and Kris.

Chapter 4

It was Friday night after supper, eight days since Fred had passed away, and Kris sat on the front step. The smell of the blueberries was gone, but he enjoyed the fragrance of the freshly cut grass that lay spread across the front yard. Allison came out of the house and sat down next to him, placed her left hand in his right, letting their entwined fingers rest upon his knee.

"I haven't even had a chance to thank you for all you've done around here this past week, Kris," Allison said softly, then laid her head on his shoulder. "We would have been lost without you."

"No need to thank me, I'm just glad I was able to be here to help," Kris said as he turned his head towards her and kissed her forehead.

Their love from previous lifetimes had been renewed,

both knew it, but neither spoke of it. They sat quietly for some time, Allison wanting to speak but not finding the courage or words to do so. Her mind was in a hundred places, her heart full of a thousand questions.

Kris finally spoke, "Go ahead and ask, it won't hurt you. I can feel something inside you wanting to come out."

Allison never moved, just stayed where she was, leaning against Kris. She spoke quietly, "That's what I'm thinking about, Kris. You. You knew I wanted to say something. You always seem to know everything before it happens. And you knew about my dad dying. You knew the night before he died what was going to happen. That's why you asked Todd and me to go to his room. How did you know it? and why did you know it?"

"Sometimes things are very easy to see. The closer we are to a situation the harder it is to see sometimes. When I arrived last week, I just knew. Your father waited for you to come home from school. He just had to see you with his eyes one more time. You were a very special child to him, for many reasons."

Allison wanted to ask why, but she didn't. She was almost afraid to. Kris always had an answer for every question and she wasn't ready yet for this answer. It was an eerie feeling, and it frightened her away from the subject. The thoughts continued to tumble through her mind. "Kris, you always make everything sound so simple when I talk to you. Then, when I start thinking about it on my own, I always get confused."

"Ah . . . life is pretty simple, but we sometimes tend to tangle things up pretty bad. The longer we are here upon this earth the easier we find that life is to live. Experience is the key. Just learn from every single thing that you do, and life becomes very easy to live. That's all there is to it."

Lifting her head from Kris' shoulder, Allison looked into his eyes. "You say that like you're pretty sure of yourself. Is that the voice of experience speaking?"

Kris stood up and gently pulled Allison to her feet. They walked hand in hand up the front walk to the sidewalk, then turned and walked up the street. The sidewalk was dark and the streetlight from the corner, several hundred feet ahead, blinked through the trees as they walked.

"Kris, you didn't answer my question," Allison said, wrapping both her arms around Kris' left arm as they walked. "Are you speaking from experience, or is that just your opinion?"

"Experience . . . I guess," Kris said weakly.

Allison looked up at Kris as they walked. "You seem to know a lot for someone your age. Does this experience come from anything you can talk about?"

Kris stopped, faced Allison, placed his arms around her waist, then spoke, "I don't know . . . it's just hard to describe . . . I've stood upon this earth and I've hurt so deep . . . so deep down inside that I thought it would never end. I've hurt so bad at times that I couldn't even stand to live with myself, and it was the most welcome thought on earth to think that I could die. I felt like I had hurt so much, so deep, for so long, that no one should ever have to hurt again, that no man, woman, or child should ever have to hurt again for the rest of eternity. I would have sworn that I had hurt enough for all of them."

Tears started to run down Kris' cheeks. "And dear God . . . Allison, I've been so lost . . . I've been more lost than a child's first conscious thought, more lost than your first penny earned and spent. It's amazing how lost a person can be, yet at the same time know where he is. I've felt more crushed inside than a flower that has been pressed between the pages of a huge and heavy book for thousands of years.

"I've been so lost, so alone, so crushed, so hurt, that I thought I'd never make it through another minute of life . . . and I guess a couple of times I didn't . . . but in the end I survived.

"I've stood here so alone, so desperate, so empty that I ached to feel someone's . . . anyone's, arms around me, but they never came . . . yet I made it. I've stood here and have been killed a thousand times inside, each one more painful than the last, and I swore that I'd never help another person, that I'd never care about another person as long as I lived . . . I've been so tired inside, so tired of giving, so tired of caring . . . yet, I always wound up finding myself caring about someone and their problems. And I learned more about giving . . . than I ever wanted to know.

"And why have I felt this way? The reasons really don't matter anymore, all that is important is that I learned from them . . . that I learned how to love all people as a result of them. That's the important thing . . . love. When someone hurts you, or someone crushes you, the only choice you have is to love them . . . all we can do is to keep on going, keep on trying. And in the end, as a result of it all, we discover that life is easy to live."

Her heart full of compassion and understanding, Allison reached up and brushed the tears from Kris' face with her fingers. She could feel the penetrating depth of his words and the conviction with which he spoke them. Looking into his eyes, she asked, "Who are you, Kris? Why did you come here?"

Lifting his head and looking into the starlit sky, Kris answered, "Who am I? . . . just a man. Why did I come here? . . . to spend the summer with you, Allison."

Again, that eerie feeling Allison had experienced a short time earlier was now back. She was afraid to find out the answer, why Kris had come to spend the summer with her. She didn't even want to think about it, yet the warmth of his arms around her body filled her with inner strength and peace, more than she had ever experienced.

It was late Saturday morning as Kris helped Eleanor and Allison straighten the house. Julie, Allison's older sister, her husband Bob, and their daughter Amy were due to arrive at any time. Kris had met them all when Fred died, but never really had a chance to visit and talk with them.

Amy was nine, almost ten, and she had fallen in love with Kris the first time she met him. She had long, blond hair, blue eyes, and the face of an angel. Amy was a victim of muscular dystrophy at the age of six months. Her legs were in steel braces and she could not walk without crutches. To move around, she had to move her crutches forward, drag her legs to a standing position, then move her crutches forward again. Moving about was a slow process for Amy, but she seldom complained. She tried to follow Kris every place he went, and was usually successful.

Amy always enjoyed coming to her grandparents' house because of the bluebirds that nested in the back yard. Fred had built several birdhouses for them years before, and once they established themselves, they returned every year. Amy would sit out in the backyard on the grass for hours watching them fly in and out of their houses.

When Julie and her family arrived, Amy only sat still

for about ten minutes, then asked if she could go out in the backyard to watch the bluebirds. Since the family had business to discuss as a result of Fred's death Kris said that he would take her out in the backyard. He picked up Amy in his right arm, grabbed the crutches and carried her out through the kitchen and down the steps into the backyard.

In the shade of a large oak tree Amy sat in her yellow dress and watched the bluebirds' houses waiting for them to fly in or out. Kris lay on his back with a long weed in his mouth staring up through the branches of the tree.

From over the roof of the garage came a half dozen yellow butterflies fluttering about in a circular pattern. "Oh look, Kris," Amy cried in excitement, "look at the pretty butterflies. Ooooh, I've never seen a butterfly up close. They're so pretty, and so tiny."

Watching the butterflies flying about the yard, Kris commented very calmly to Amy, "Why not ask them to come over and see you. You don't have to ask them with words, just tell them with your heart and mind, they'll hear you. Just tell them that you love them, that they're pretty and that you will not harm them. And if you really mean what you tell them, then they will come to you. Just stretch your arms out so they will have a place to land."

Amy looked at Kris with a half-believing expression on her face, yet her heart was full of trust as she reached out her arms. Kris could see her lips move slightly as she talked to the butterflies. They came closer and closer and soon they all landed on her outstretched arms.

"They did it, Kris!" Amy whispered excitedly, "they did it!"

"What'd I tell you, Amy."

Then from over the garage, and hedges, and house,

and through the yard came butterflies. Yellow ones, blue ones, striped ones, white ones. They came by the dozens and they lit on Amy's arms, fingers, hair, and legs. They clung to her dress and landed on her shoes. The air was full of butterflies. She laughed out loud and giggled, and the butterflies laughed with her.

"Look at me, Kris! Look at them all around me," Amy said as she moved her arms back and forth in a circular, swinging motion. As she moved her arms, some would lose their balance, flutter away, then return.

Kris sat up slowly and asked, "And how about the bluebirds? Would you like to see them too?"

"Oh yes, yes, yes," she cried in excitement.

Kris outstretched his arms and from out of the bird-houses came bluebirds, thirty bluebirds flying as fast as they could come. They landed on his arms, shoulders, head, and hands.

And there they sat, laughing and carrying on with bluebirds and butterflies flying around them, and sitting all over their bodies.

Julie walked into the kitchen to get a drink of water. She removed a glass from the cupboard, stood at the sink and filled it with water. As she raised the glass to her mouth she looked out the window and saw Amy and Kris sitting on the grass, surrounded by, and covered with what appeared to be hundreds of birds and butterflies. Julie gasped as she took the glass from her lips and put it in the sink. She headed out the back door and down the steps as fast as her legs would carry her. As she approached, Kris looked at her, puckered up his lips, and softly said, "Shhhhhh, quiet."

Amy cried out, "Look Mommy, look at the birds and butterflies! Look at them Mommy! They love me!"

Julie sat down on the grass about ten feet away, her

mouth open in astonishment, her eyes not believing what she saw. Kris looked at her with a smile in his eyes that was much bigger than the one on his face. Julie could not speak.

For five more minutes Julie watched as the two were surrounded by the flying beauty. Finally, Amy said, "Kris, my arms are getting tired. How do I get them to leave?"

"Just thank them for coming, for sharing their beauty and love. Tell them that they can now be on their way."

Kris and Amy both thanked them with their minds and heart, and as quickly as they came, so they left.

"Mama! Mama! Did you see them?" Amy asked in excitement. Julie just nodded, still too shocked to say anything.

"How did they do that, Kris?" Amy asked, "How did you know that they would come?"

"A little *true love* goes a long way, Amy. Everything responds to real love."

"You mean any animal would come to me?" Amy asked even more excitedly.

"Sure, and they won't hurt you. I don't care if it is a rattlesnake, a lion, tiger, a bear, you name it. They'll all come and love you just like the butterflies and birds. As long as they know that you will not harm them and you just want to share with them, they'll all come. If an animal doesn't come, or is slow in coming, it is because they already have had some bad experience with a human. But soon they will come. Eventually, everything must respond to love." Kris paused for a few seconds, then said in a voice that reflected back upon many years, "I guess the hardest thing to get to respond to love is people. We are always so suspicious about why someone is so nice to us or cares about us. But, eventually we learn what it is all about."

Amy squinted up her nose into a look of questioning disbelief, and asked, "Do you mean that even a wild animal, like a bear, that goes around tearing everything apart would even come to me and not hurt me?"

"Oh, in time it would. Sometimes animals get sick and they're a little harder to deal with than others. But what usually happens is, that as they come closer in response to love, you get scared, and the closer they come the more scared you get, and pretty soon you are frightened, then they get frightened, then who knows what happens."

Julie sat by listening, interested in what Kris was saying, but not really believing it. It was a good Sunday School story to tell a young child, but not beneficial to an adult.

Kris looked into Amy's innocent face, a little girl already full of love, and continued, "You know, Amy, God never creates anything imperfectly. A bug may eat a rose bud, or a worm may eat a tomato, but when they were both created, they were perfect. And the worms and bugs are also perfect creations. What this means is, that everything must live in harmony with everything else."

Amy dropped her head slightly and looked at her legs, not more than an inch or so in diameter, covered by steel braces and leather straps. "Didn't God create me imperfectly?"

Kris scooted closer to Amy. "Do you think that God would create one of His highest creations imperfectly? He would never do that. He gave us perfect life and it is *us* that causes undesirable things to happen. The God I know would never do anything to hurt anyone."

"Well, what did I do to make my legs like this? Mama said my legs have always been like this."

"Amy, there are a lot of things to learn while we are

on this earth. So many, in fact, that there isn't enough time to learn them all in one lifteime. So we have to live here many, many times to learn them all."

"Do you mean I'll live again?" Amy said with her nose all squished-up once again.

"Yes, and you have already lived a great number of times, but you don't remember them. You see, everything lives over and over again. Look at the apple. It grows on a tree, falls to the ground, rots, seeds take root in the ground, and it lives again, the very same apple. See, everything dies and lives again.

"But, Amy, we are more than apples, an animal, or plant, and we do more than just eat and grow. Our lives involve the lives of others and all those things that we do to them, and that they do to us. So when we die on this earth, just like your Grandpa did, we, or our soul, goes to a place and we kind-of relive our life, looking at it to see what we did wrong and what we did right. Those things that we did wrong we will have to relive again in another time. And hopefully, the next time we will try and do them the right way."

Amy sat engrossed in what Kris was saying. She sat perfectly still, listening carefully not to miss a single word.

Kris continued, "You see, if we kill someone, then in some other lifetime we will be killed by someone else. If we hurt people, then we will be hurt. It's that simple. But there is a way, when we do something wrong, that we won't have to suffer what we did to another, and that is to learn while we are still on the earth that what we did was wrong. And if we see that we were wrong after we did something, and we never do that again, or any other similar thing, then we don't have to suffer, because what we have learned has changed our lives. So the important thing is to learn from everything we do.

"And once we learn all the things that there are to know about love, then we don't have to come back here . . . unless we want to. You see, after we learn all the lessons of love we are free to make a choice: either continue our learning in other places beyond the earth, or we can come back here and help those that we love to learn their lessons. And sometimes souls are so full of love that they just keep coming back to help others, and to share, and to be with those they love very deeply."

Amy looked down at her legs again, then asked, "What you said earlier about hurting people . . . do you mean that I hurt someone's legs once?"

Kris looked her straight in the eyes, "Yes, I believe you did, that is why you are like this today."

Julie grew furious inside because she could see that Amy was getting upset, even a little scared. She wanted to ask Kris to stop, but the words would not form in her mouth and she was forced to sit silently. She struggled to move, but she couldn't.

Amy's face was long and drawn. She asked Kris, "Do you know what I did to someone a long time ago? . . . I mean to their legs?"

Kris reached out and took Amy's hands, the physical diary from which her soul's past experiences could be read. He could tell that her soul had lived over three hundred times and was well on her way to finishing her life trips. Her hands filled his mind with many visions of her past lives and soon he focused-in on what Amy had asked.

"Amy, a little over two thousand years ago you were a soldier in the Roman army. You were very brave and fought in a great number of battles. You were friends with another soldier and you were very close to each other. You fought side by side many times. In one battle an enemy soldier killed your friend and you became insanely mad. You took your sword and struck the enemy soldier in the back of his legs, cutting his muscles. But you did not strike him just once, but over and over again, cutting his legs to pieces . . . ."

Julie was screaming inside for Kris to stop, but she could not move nor talk. Something inside held her prisoner where she sat.

". . . And as a result of what you did the man could never walk again. You did not physically kill him, but you killed him inside, in his heart and mind. The man lost his dignity and pride. He had to crawl and be carried every place he went, and he became full of hate and bitterness.

"You see, Amy, to die in the physical body is not so bad, but to die inside is one of the most miserable deaths a person can suffer."

Tears poured from Amy's eyes. She sniffled and wiped the tears away with the sleeve of her dress. "Did I really do that, Kris?" she asked, trying to hold back the tears.

"Yes you did. I wouldn't have told you that if you hadn't . . . . Did you learn anything from it, Amy?"

"Oh yes, yes, yes, Kris. I would never, ever hurt anyone again. Not in any way, never," Amy said in a crying and sincere voice.

Kris took her hands again, "Not to hurt means more than just physically hurting someone. You see, our body can heal most of the time. *It's our words and actions that do the most damage.* So not to hurt also means not to say mean or unnecessary things. Do you see that?"

"Oh yes, Kris, yes I do," Amy said anxiously. And as

she spoke, her hands reflected the growth she had just experienced.

"Well, Amy, that's the important thing, that we learn from it all," Kris said as he moved over next to Amy's legs. "Amy, I'm going to lift your dress up a little and take these braces off your legs . . . okay?"

"Why, Kris? Why?" Amy asked in a scared, almost shivering voice.

"Well, now that you have learned from what you did wrong there is no reason to wear these things anymore. You will be able to walk without them, now."

Julie's inside screamed at Kris to stop, to leave her child alone, that all of this had gone too far, but she still could not move or say anything.

As Kris unbuckled the leather straps he continued talking. "Amy, do you know who the man you hurt was?"

"No," Amy said as she nervously watched Kris work at removing her braces.

"Well, he forgave you, and today loves you very much. Today that person you hurt is a woman, just like you are, and I'll tell you who she is," Kris said as he looked at Amy, "it's your mother. She loves you so much that she wanted to be with you to help you through your hardship . . . but that's all over now," he said as he unfastened the last strap.

Kris slid the left brace off first. As he did so he passed his hand over her leg. Then the right leg. Amy stared at her legs while Kris picked up the braces and threw them aside.

Kris sat back, then said with a certain authority in his voice, yet calm and compassionate, "Now get up and walk, Amy."

"Help me up, Kris," Amy cried.

"No. If you're going to walk, get up and do it your-self. From this moment on you will never need anyone's help to ever walk again."

Amy rolled over on to her stomach and pushed her-self upright, standing on her knees as she was used to doing with her braces. She then took her left leg and lifted it, bringing her left foot to rest on the ground. Then her right foot. She was standing by herself! She turned around and faced her mother. Julie rose to her knees. Amy took one step towards her mother, then another, then another. "Mommy, Mommy," she cried, "I can walk! I can walk!"

She walked four more steps and Amy and her mother embraced each other. They both cried aloud, tears streaming from their faces while Kris *indifferently* worked at disassembling Amy's aluminum crutches.

"Amy," Kris interrupted, "the first thing I want you to do now that you can walk is to pick up these braces and crutches and go put them in the garbage cans behind the garage.

Amy left her mother, walked over, picked up the braces and crutches, then walked slowly, disappearing behind the garage. Kris could hear the garbage can being opened, the metal objects drop inside, then the cover placed back on the can. A few seconds later Amy emerged from behind the garage running at full tilt. She jumped, flapped her arms, and laughed out loud. As she ran towards Kris and Julie she fell down, rolled over onto her back, laughing and kicking the ground. She ran to Julie and gave her another big hug, then ran the few steps to Kris. "I love you, Kris," she cried, "I love you!"

Kris pushed her back a little, then asked, "Now that you can walk, what do you want to do?"

"First I want to go show Daddy and Grandma, and

Todd and Allison. Then I want to go to the park and swing on the swings, and play on the teeter-totter. And I want to run and push the merry-go-round around in circles. I've always wanted to do that. I want to get all the kids in the whole park together and put them on the merry-go-round . . . . and let me push them around in circles!"

"Then go inside, Amy, and show everyone that you can walk. Then you and I will walk down to the park."

Amy took off running for the house as fast as she could go. Julie and Kris stood and watched as Amy climbed the stairs and went inside. Julie wanted to be with Amy so she could see the expressions on Bob and Eleanor's face, but something was more important than that. She turned and looked at Kris. "Kris, who are you? and why did you come here this summer?"

"I'm just a man, and I came to try and bring a little love."

Chapter 5

It was Saturday evening and the four of them had just finished eating dinner. Allison, Eleanor, Todd and Kris sat at the table looking at each other. Julie, Amy and Bob had left a short time earlier. Julie and Bob drove the nine-tenths of a mile to their house, while Amy walked the distance. She had insisted that she walk it by herself.

Eleanor sat at the head of the table with her arms crossed, elbows resting on the table. She would look over at Kris then glance down at her empty plate. Allison and Todd could feel the tension from their mother. They both got up and began to clear the table. Eleanor and Kris remained seated. As Allison and Todd disappeared into the kitchen Eleanor could hold it inside no longer. "Kris," she said, "who are you and why did you come here this summer?"

"Why?" Kris answered, "does something about me bother you?"

"Yes," Eleanor said in a calm voice, "yes it does. Almost everything about you bothers me. I don't think I've ever met a nicer man than you, and that includes Fred, God rest his soul. And I don't know what I would have done if you hadn't been here when he died. But something about you still bothers me. Today, with the butterflies and bluebirds . . . Julie told me all about it. Then that story you told to Amy about the soldiers, and then her walking . . . I just can't believe it. It's not possible . . . or is it? Was it a miracle?"

"Oh, some may call it that," Kris said softly, "but it's just a matter of believing."

"And what will Amy's doctor say? Dr. Moser will never believe it. Will it last? Will Amy ever need crutches or braces again?"

"No." Kris replied. "Amy will never again need crutches or braces as long as she lives. And the muscles in her legs will develop very quickly. She'll have beautiful, normal legs soon." Kris looked at Eleanor and smiled, "Now what else about me is bothering you?"

"Just little things. Like how you get all of the clothes you wear out of that little bag of yours. You haven't bought anything since you've been here, yet your closet is full. You had two different suits . . . you wore one at the funeral home and one at Fred's funeral. You have work clothes, dress clothes, everything you need. Where did they come from?

"And your money . . . you've paid me rent twice now, both times you gave me two new twenty dollar bills and that's all there was in your wallet. Then three days ago when you and I went to the grocery store . . . you bought some things that cost three dollars and eighty-seven cents. You opened your wallet and took out three new, one dollar bills, then reached in your pocket and pulled out eighty-seven cents in new coins and laid them on the counter. I mean, you didn't pull out a pocket full of change and count out eighty-seven cents, you just pulled it out of your pocket like it was all the money you had. Then, not five minutes later we were at the drug store and you needed a dollar and seventeen cents. What did you do? You opened your wallet and pulled out a dollar bill, one that was not there five minutes earlier, then reached in your pocket and pulled out seventeen cents in new coins. You didn't count it, just pulled it out of your pocket like before."

In a calm, cool voice Kris said, "Guess I'm just fortunate and happen to have everything I'll ever need."

Eleanor looked at him disbelieving, then continued, "Kris, do you have a drivers license?"

"Uh, drivers license? . . . yeah, sure," Kris said hesitantly as he removed his wallet from his rear pocket. He opened it. Eleanor observed that there was no paper money in it as he did so. He unsnapped the leather tab that held the accordian style plastic inserts designed to hold credit cards and pictures. They were all empty except one which contained his drivers license. He removed it and handed it to Eleanor.

As she looked at it, Eleanor noticed that the date of birth had been conveniently smudged so that it could not be read. Otherwise, the license enclosed in laminated plastic looked just like hers. She gave it back to Kris and as he folded the plastic inserts back into place and snapped the compartment shut, Eleanor asked, "Kris, do you have a Social Security Card?"

"Sure," he said and started to unsnap the compartment again, then caught himself, "yeah, I have one, but it's up in my room."

A big smile spread across Eleanor's face. "Are you

sure one just didn't appear in your wallet?" she said in almost a sarcastic voice.

"Yes, I'm sure. It is up in my room in the dresser drawer."

Eleanor pushed herself away from the table then said with a smile, "Kris, I'd trust you with my life, I'd do anything for you, and I have a special love for you, but something about you still bothers me. Perhaps it bothers me because I can't understand, or because I find it difficult to believe what I know I should believe."

As she stood up, Kris reached out and took Eleanor by the hand, then said, "Eleanor, promise me that you'll tell me when I stop bothering you."

They smiled at each other with respect, then Eleanor began picking up the dishes from the table. They all worked together to clean the table and wash the dishes.

Kris sat on the top step of the back porch and Allison sat two steps down lower, leaning back against his legs. They sat looking out across the back yard and watched the full, snow-white moon rise above the silhouetted trees. Stars shown brightly, twinkling throughout the nighttime sky. They sat quietly for a long time.

Kris looked down at Allison and spoke softly, "It'll be raining by morning."

"Think so?"

"Yeah. The front is moving in from the west. It'll be here by three o'clock in the morning. Need to wear your raincoat to church."

"Are you going to go with us?"

"No, I don't think so."

They sat together quietly again for some time enjoying the silence and each other's presence. The moon had risen a little higher into the sky and the stars shown brighter than ever.

"Kris?" Allison asked.

"Yes."

"Are those things that my mother was saying at the dinner table true? I didn't mean to be eavesdropping, but I couldn't help hearing what was being said. Is it true about the money and your clothes? I never really paid any attention."

"Yeah, I guess they are true. But you have to remember . . . things appear differently to different people. We generally tend to get scared of things we don't understand, so I can understand your mother's apprehension."

"Kris, last night you told me that you came to spend the summer with me. Why did you say that?"

Placing his hands on Allison's shoulders, Kris gently squeezed her back with his thumbs. "Only because it's true. What I told Amy today about living over and over again . . . well, it's true. You and I have walked this earth many times together, and I just had to come and be with you one more time. I can only stay the summer and you'll never see me again in this lifetime. I love you, Allison, that's all I can say," then pressed his face into her hair, kissing her head.

Allison turned and looked up at Kris, "And without me saying a word you know how I feel about you, right?"

"Yes, just don't grow to depend on me too much because I will be leaving by the end of the summer."

"Why, Kris? Why must you leave? Why can't you stay longer?"

Kris sighed deeply, "It's so easy for me to see, yet so hard to explain. All I can say is that I was permitted to come here this summer . . . to spend it with you. It's been so long since we were together on this earth that I just had to be with you. Between our lifetimes I am with you constantly, but it's been many lifetimes since we've been together. I live on earth every now and then to fulfill some commitments I have made to other souls, but my real love is with you.

"Allison, you might say that I'm indirectly bound to this earth for several thousand more years because of the commitments I have made, and since I am, every now and then I would just like to be with you, to spend some time with you."

"Kris, I really can't say that I know what you are talking about, but I'm trying to."

"It's really not important that you understand. The only real thing that we both need to understand is that I will be leaving soon. No exceptions can be made about this."

Kris watched as Allison nodded her head, "Maybe I'll understand later . . . but for now just hold my hand and let me share and enjoy your strength and wisdom."

As they continued watching the moon, the first small, puffy clouds from the approaching front drifted in from the western sky.

Chapter 6

It was Thursday of the following week and the medical profession in town was a little upset about Amy's healing. The town's weekly newspaper, published every Wednesday, carried quite an article about Amy, and also Kris. A lot of crank calls were made to the Haynes' home as well as a lot of serious ones from other people who were looking and searching to be cured of sickness. Many people came by on Wednesday afternoon and evening looking for Kris but he was nowhere to be found. No one knew where he was.

It was after 1:00 A.M. when the last of the seekers gave up and went home. As the last car drove away, Kris emerged from under the drooping branches of one of the large weeping willow trees and walked up onto the front porch.

The Chicago branch of the AMA had also heard of

Amy's healing and were forming a delegation to come and see Kris. No matter how often they came, Kris was never found at home.

Wednesday had also been Todd's last day of school and this Thursday morning found him standing out on the curb looking skyward, watching a small private plane from the nearby airport fly overhead.

Kris walked out the front door, down the walk and stood beside Todd. "Todd, do you like flying?"

"Yes, I think I would. I've never been up in an airplane, but I've always wanted to. I really think I'd like to be a pilot."

"Flying has changed a lot since I used to fly . . . they have all that electronic stuff now."

"You mean you know how to fly, Kris?"

"Sure . . . it's been years ago. Say would you like to go for a ride?"

"Golly yeah . . . when?"

"How about now? Let's go see if we can borrow the car from your mother and we'll head out to the airport."

The local airport wasn't much more than a cow pasture with about twenty airplanes sitting around. Runways were of grass with occasional bare spots here and there. The two hangars were old barns, and on the one small building that looked most likely to collapse at any moment hung a bright new sign: FLIGHT OPERATIONS HEADQUARTERS. Todd had told Kris that the airport was run by a couple of old World War II fighter pilots.

Kris pushed hard against the door of the flight operations headquareters building until it finally broke loose from its jammed position. Inside, the walls were covered with old, dusty pictures of every conceivable kind of aircraft. Old tires, bent propellors, pieces of airplanes and fabric cluttered the small room. Two men in their early fifties, both wearing blue baseball caps, flannel shirts and bib overalls sat among the rubble. One sat with his feet propped up on a small, round table stacked high with aviation magazines, the other sitting behind the counter drinking a coke from a bottle. The one behind the counter stood up and said, "Hi there young fella. My name's Bimbo, and that offensive looking cuss over there is Nat. Can we help you?"

"Yes, yes you can. I'm Kris and this is Todd. I'd like to rent an airplane for a couple of hours for some local flying."

Bimbo rested his right elbow on the counter top, then pushed his hat a little further back on his head with his right hand. "You got a license young fella?"

"Yeah . . . sure," Kris replied a little hesitantly.

"Can I see it?"

Kris removed his wallet and unsnapped the leather compartment containing the plastic inserts. He removed a reduced photostat copy of a document and handed it to Bimbo.

Bimbo looked it over very carefully. "Say, you've done a heap of flying haven't you? Multi-engine, instrument, flight instructor. Hey, you've got 'em all, don't you?"

"Yeah, I guess."

Bimbo handed the license back to Kris. "Alright, now what do you want to fly?"

"How about that Cessna 172 sitting out there."

"Okay. That'll be fifteen dollars an hour. You go out and pre-flight it and then I'll need to take you up for a check ride. I'll be out in a minute."

Kris and Todd went outside and began to pre-flight the airplane. Kris explained everything he was doing to Todd as he checked the engine, fuel, wings, ailerons, flaps, and tail. In a few minutes Bimbo came out of the shack, walked over and put his arm around Todd. "Okay son, you stay here until we get back. We won't be gone but a few minutes."

With Bimbo and Kris inside the airplane, Kris started the engine. As he taxied the airplane to the end of the runway Kris placed the flight check list on his right knee and worked his way down through it in the manner of a seasoned professional. Near the end of the runway he stopped the airplane, revved the engine checking the magnetos and carburetor heat, set the gyro compass to agree with the magnetic compass and moved out onto the runway. He advanced the throttle to about three-fourths power and the plane started to move forward. It hadn't moved much more than fifty feet or so when Kris hauled back on the wheel and the airplane started to climb almost straight up. Bimbo reached out, grabbing onto the dash board and yelled, "You're gonna kill us boy, you're gonna kill us!"

The plane continued to climb near vertical at a low power setting. "Relax Bimbo, relax," Kris said calmly as he leveled off at eight hundred feet, checked for nearby aircraft, than turned away from the airport. "Now what do you want me to show you, Bimbo?"

"Noth . . . ing, nothing," Bimbo stammered, his face snow white. "If you can get us back to the ground in one piece . . . that'll be enough."

Bimbo walked into the operations building as Kris and Todd took off. Nat looked up at Bimbo and said, "My God, Bimbo, what's wrong? You look like you've seen a ghost!"

"No," Bimbo said. "I didn't see one, I just flew with one." He walked over and finished the coke he was drinking in one swallow. "Something about that guy ain't right," he said almost muttering to himself. "He did things with that airplane that are impossible. We should have been killed."

"What are you talking about? Say, you been drinking in the morning again?" Nat asked Bimbo in a familiar voice.

"Listen, Nat, I'm telling you, some'n ain't right about that Kris fella. We took off in less than fifty feet and we weren't even at full throttle . . . then we climbed straight up. And when we landed he didn't even use the runway! We landed right out here next to this shack, not a hundred feet from here. He side-slipped it all the way in, and we didn't even roll ten feet when we hit the ground."

"Now wait a minute, Bimbo," Nat said jumping to his feet, "you expect me to believe that? You've been drinking, haven't you? Bimbo, you've got to stop that stuff!"

"Now shut up, Nat! Listen. You know how the plane always vibrates when you fly? You know, the plane always bounces a little. Well, with this guy its like the plane was sitting on the ground. It was perfectly smooth. It didn't seem right, so I took the controls for a minute, and as soon as I did, the plane started its normal vibration. When he took the controls back, it got smooth again." Nat looked at Bimbo with questioning eyes, "Listen, Bimbo . . . ."

"Nat, I told you to shut up. Listen . . . hear that?" Bimbo said as he cocked his head towards the door. "What's that guy doing?"

In the distance could be heard the whine and roar that an aircraft engine makes to listeners on the ground as it performs aerobatic stunts. Nat and Bimbo went outside. They looked across the field and through squinting eyes they could see the Cessna 172 performing loops, a split-S and a Cuban-8. "Dag-nab-it!" Bimbo shouted as he jumped up and down, then threw his hat to the ground. He cupped his hands around his mouth and yelled at the plane as if Kris could hear, "Stop that! Stop that young fella! That plane ain't meant to fly like that!" Bimbo turned to Nat, "When he gets down we're both gonna go flying with him. You'll see I'm not crazy."

In the airplane Kris was giving instructions to Todd, perhaps in an unorthodox manner, but very effective. Todd listened closely as Kris talked, and like most people, he really didn't completely understand everything that Kris said, but he tried.

"You see, Todd, flying isn't really any different than doing anything else. The real secret is to talk to the airplane with your mind and heart, then listen to what it has to say to you. When you don't feel any response from it or something doesn't feel right, then don't try it. Your hands must be extra sensitive on the controls, feeling, listening to what the airplane has to say.

"Now let's try a slow roll to the left. A little left rudder and wheel together to get us into the roll . . . feel the nose want to drop as we start to become inverted? . . . just a little forward pressure on the wheel to correct that . . . now a little right aileron and rudder as we come back to horizontal . . . see, that's all there is to it.

"You see . . . it is not man and machine, or man and airplane. You are not two separate things . . . when you are flying you are one. Your hands don't stop at the wheel, they extend to the ailerons and elevator on the tail . . . in fact, they are the ailerons and elevator. The same with your feet . . . your feet become the rudder. When you want to do something all you need to do is think it and the airplane will respond, for it is now a part of you. And once you master flying according to the principles of aerodynamic laws known to man, you will discover how to fly according to the laws of the mind.

"And another thing . . . you must never push an airplane, or anything for that matter, to its limits. Never slam the throttle wide open and hold it there for any extended period of time. Never jerk the controls around. You must treat an airplane, or car, your bicycle, or your home . . . you must treat everything with love and respect. Treat everything in your life like it is the woman you love. And how do you treat the woman you love? You treat her gently, with respect, caring . . . you would never do anything to hurt her or deceive her . . . you would do nothing to harm her in any way. Therefore, treat everything with love, feeling, respect, and concern. Become one, become unified with everything you come in contact with . . . then you have nothing to fear from whatever or whomever you deal with."

At the end of two hours Todd was performing every trick in the book with perfection. It was a perfect demonstration that thinking it, made it so. Kris brought the airplane in for a landing again near the operations shack. Bimbo and Nat watched through the window. As the plane neared the ground they both could be heard making a hissing sound as they inhaled deeply through gritted teeth, awaiting the impending crash. They both turned their heads away from the window as the plane came close to the ground, and held their breath awaiting the sound of the explosive crash. After a few seconds they peeked through the window again only to see that the plane had landed and rolled to a stop in the tie-down spot where Kris had pre-flighted the aircraft two hours earlier.

Kris walked into the operations shack and gave Bimbo the thirty dollars. Bimbo wanted to ask a hundred questions but couldn't find the words to ask a single one. Kris thanked the men, then left.

Bimbo watched as they drove off. He raised his eyebrows high, at the same time squinting his eyes closed and murmured to himself, "Who are you boy, who are you?" Bimbo sat down and picked up Wednesday's newspaper, unfolded it, then looked at the front page where he saw Amy's picture. The related story told of Amy's healing and the strange young man in town that prompted this miracle. Jumping to his feet Bimbo shouted, "Did you see this paper, Nat? Do you see this story?" he said as he jabbed his finger into the front page, "I told you something was strange about that guy!"

It was just about lunch time when Kris and Todd got back into town from the airport. As they turned the corner and headed towards the house they could see cars parked all along both sides of the street, and a large group of people standing in front of the house out on the sidewalk. Kris turned into the driveway and drove back to the garage behind the house. Eleanor and Allison came out of the back door, down the steps, and walked to the car.

Looking at Allison, then Eleanor, Kris said, "Guess I know why everyone's here. I'm sorry Eleanor, I didn't mean to cause all of this. I know that all of this doesn't help you any . . . I mean, I know you're still upset about Fred, and . . . well, all this commotion just isn't helping. I'll go out front and talk to them," he said, then started down the driveway.

Eleanor reached out taking Kris by the arm and stopped him. "Don't you want anything to eat first? You may be out there all afternoon."

"No thanks," Kris replied, turned and continued down the driveway.

Kris rounded the corner of the house and looked at the group of sixty or more people filled with those on crutches, in wheel-chairs, with canes, and those that limped and hobbled. It was almost like a mob scene as they rushed towards him, all grabbing and pulling at him. Kris pushed his way to the front step and stood looking out over the crowd. His dark eyes seemed to focus on each person, and without saying a word the crowd became quiet.

One by one he took individuals and families aside speaking with them. They were all after the same thing: a healing back to perfect health. They all wanted a short cut to feeling good again. Kris tried to explain that while they could be healed now, *unless they corrected the real cause of the problem,* it or another sickness would return again shortly. He tried to tell them that they must be willing to work with the cause first, rather than the cure, for *the cure was in the cause.* None of them would listen. He could understand their impatience, but he tried to explain that law only works according to law. He told them that before any situation can be improved, you must first rise above it and learn from it, but they refused to listen.

And to those that he explained the cause of their problems, they also refused to listen. To them it was be healed now; nothing else would do. And one by one they left, each calling him a hoax, a charlatan, a fake.

It was six o'clock when the last of the people left, each murmuring discontent under their breath. As the last car pulled away Kris looked up the sidewalk and saw a man and woman dressed in shabby clothes standing next to an old '53, rusted-out Chevy with Ohio license plates. Sitting in front of them was a young retarded and deformed girl in an old wheelchair made from weaved

wicker with wooden wheels. The man was hunched over a
little and wore an old worn-out suit with no tie. The lady
had on an old sack dress, her black hair matted down.
Within her was a strong inherent beauty, and it was
obvious that she was a matured woman.

As Kris walked towards them the man stepped away
from his wife and child and walked towards Kris. As he
got closer Kris could see the man's face filled with pain
each time he took a step. When they reached each other
they shook hands. "Are you Kris?" the man asked.

"Yes, I'm Kris McDaniels."

"I'm George Preston. We heard about you on the
news Tuesday night. We drove all day yesterday and all
last night from eastern Ohio to come and see you . . . to
see if you could help our daughter, Marjorie."

George and Kris walked slowly towards the car. As
they walked, George continued, "Marjorie was born retarded and deformed. The doctors say there is nothing
that can be done to help her. Things weren't too bad
until about five years ago when I fell off a roof and broke
my back. It's hard for me to move sometimes and I just
can't seem to hold a job. We're on welfare but most of
our money goes to Marjorie for special food and medicine
. . . see, she can't chew food, so we have to give her a
special formula."

Kris stopped about ten feet from the car. "You say
you drove all day and night to get here?"

George nodded. "Yes, yes we did. The car doesn't run
too good anymore and it took us quite a while to get
here. My wife, Mary, had to do all the driving. I just can't
sit behind the wheel and drive . . . it just hurts so much.
In fact . . . I don't even know how we're going to get
home . . . we only have two dollars left.

"We came here on blind faith hoping that you could

help her. We've been to everyone we could find, but no one has been able to help . . . uh, uh, Mr. McDaniels, can you help? I mean I've seen all these people leave just the same as they came."

Kris stopped and looked at George, "I'll see if I can help. No promises." Kris hesitated, then asked, "Ah, George, do you want to be healed also? Do you want your back healed?"

"Well, no. I hadn't even thought about that. I just want Marjorie to be okay."

Kris walked over and introduced himself to Mary, then squatted down and looked at Marjorie. She was fourteen, with very short brown hair, eyes dark and recessed deep within her head, teeth crooked and misplaced from lack of use. Her skin was snow white, arms skinny, hands folded into fists that never opened, and her left leg was about three inches shorter than her right.

Taking hold of Marjorie's hand Kris could tell that her condition was not caused by anything that she had done in her previous lives. She had only come to earth with this condition to learn humility and patience. Her learning was about over and she would die within the next year unless something happened to let her learn more. Her parents had learned patience, understanding, compassion, and love to its fullest degree.

Standing up, Kris looked at the couple and said, "I'll see what I can do."

George stepped closer and spoke, "You see, we just couldn't put her in a home. If they could help her it would be different. But they would only feed her and bathe her . . . and we can do that . . . and besides," George continued as the tears streamed from his eyes, "she's our daughter."

Reaching down, Kris unfastened the two leather belts

that held Marjorie upright in the wheelchair. He picked her up into his arms and held her seventy pound body like she was a new born baby. He leaned his head forward and kissed her forehead. He took his right hand and rubbed it across her face and down her arms and legs. As George and Mary watched they saw Marjorie's left leg grow to the length of her right leg. He kissed her face and her recessed eyes brightened. She smiled and her teeth were straight, her hands unfolded for the first time in her life as she reached up and touched Kris' face.

Kris lowered her gently and stood her on the sidewalk. George and Mary openly cried as they stepped over to hold onto Marjorie while she smiled, moved her arms about, and tried to walk. Kris released her, stepped over to the wheelchair and gave it a push up the sidewalk towards the house. He turned around and spoke to George and Mary, "Your daughter will be fine. She has the intelligence now of a child about six months old. She will progress physically and mentally very, very fast, and in about six months she will be a normal, intelligent fourteen year old girl. I suspect she will be walking within a week. She is going to observe everything that you do, so be very, very cautious in what you do and say around her. She is going to learn very quickly. Whether you know it or not, all of you have already learned a great deal in this lifetime, and now you will have the opportunity to learn even more."

They walked to the car and helped Marjorie into the back seat. Kris reached out and took Mary by the arms and kissed her on the forehead, looked into her eyes and said, "Things will change very quickly now for all of you. Enjoy yourself."

George closed the back door and stepped up to Kris, "How do I ever thank you Mr. McDaniels? What can I do?"

Just take care of your daughter. That's all I ask," Kris said, then wrapped his arms around George, giving him a hug. He stepped back a few steps, then asked, "George, why don't you drive home and give Mary a rest?"

"But my back . . . " George started to say, then realized that he was standing straight without any pain, "but . . . ."

Kris interrupted, "I'm going to take this wheelchair back to the house with me since you won't need it any more. I believe your car will make it back home without any troubles either," then turned and walked away pushing the wheelchair.

Mary and George stood with their mouths open, watching Kris as he walked up the street pushing the wheelchair. Mary got into the car and George walked around and got in behind the steering wheel. He started the engine and it purred as if it were new.

Kris parked the wheelchair next to the garbage cans where Amy had thrown her braces. He smiled because he could already see the expression on George's face when he stopped to spend his last two dollars for gas and found two hundred dollars in new twenty dollar bills in his wallet.

Chapter 7

It was late Friday morning when Allison suggested to Kris that they go down to the river, where it was quiet, for a picnic lunch. Kris had already talked with many people that morning, none of whom would listen to the truth he spoke. Allison packed a lunch after Kris agreed, and they rode bicycles the two miles to where the river crossed one of the back roads. They walked upriver for another quarter-mile or so, to a clearing of pasture that bordered the river where it was only a few feet deep.

They lay on a blanket and stared at the clear sky, occasionally at each other, and talked for over two hours, mostly about Allison and her life. Kris would casually fill in the details that she would sometimes leave out.

After lunch they lay wrapped together in the blanket as the late afternoon sky pushed the sun towards the horizon. Kris lay with his face buried in Allison's neck and shoulder when she spoke. "Kris, I don't want to go home, I could stay here in your arms forever."

61

"I know . . . I know what you mean."

"Kris? . . . ."

"Yes?"

"Promise me one thing . . . ."

"What?"

"That you'll never mention leaving here again."

Kris drew in a deep breath, then released it slowly, "Alright, I won't ever mention it again if that's what you want, but I am going to have to leave . . . and maybe sooner than I thought."

Allison lifted Kris' head away from her so she could look at his face, "Why? Why must you go?"

"I have no choice. Those were the conditions I agreed to when I came here. You have several things to learn in this life, and my being here will prevent that. We will have our opportunity to be together again when the time is right."

Allison turned her head away from Kris. "I'm sorry Kris . . . I'm so sorry, but I just don't understand. I really don't understand what you are saying. But if you must leave, why do you have to leave so early?"

"Let me try and explain it this way. Each of us . . . each man, woman, and child has the right to live their life at their own level of understanding. The key here, is understanding. Some people's understanding may appear cold, ruthless, or primitive, but this is only because they are inexperienced souls in the adventure of living on this earth. Likewise, I must live my life at my own level of understanding. What happened to Amy happened at my level of understanding, and it has caused quite a disturbance in this town. But it would have been wrong to let Amy go on as she was in order not to cause a disturbance, when I could help. But each disturbance I make will cut my time here shorter, simply because people will become uneasy with me around. So I will have to leave a little earlier. And if what I do here causes a disturbance, then I will have to cause it, because I can only do what I know is right, regardless of the consequences."

Kris rolled from his side onto his back. "Perhaps I was wrong in coming here. Perhaps I was selfish, but . . . Allison, I just wanted to be with you. I didn't want to upset you, or this town. I just wanted to be with you.

"Allison, I'm not trying to be mysterious, but the whole story of how I got here is kind of unbelievable. It happens every now and then, but it is unusual. I think that you must agree there was an instant rapport between us when we met, in fact, when we first saw each other at the bus station, right?"

"Yes . . . I can't deny that."

"You see, we were just old friends reuniting our relationship."

"Kris, I'll quit asking questions. I'm just glad you're here, and . . . I do love you, so much."

Kris rolled over and rested on his elbows, looking at Allison. He spoke softly, with a kiss in his eye, "Allison, I love you . . . I love you more than any man has ever loved any woman since the beginning of time. I know as certain as I am lying here on the ground that no man has ever walked this earth and loved a woman more than I love you. I know that a great number of men have felt the same way, and have spoken the same words to someone else, and meant it. And while they meant it from the depths of their hearts, I know that when I speak them, they are the absolute truth. Believe me, I know . . . I just know," Kris said as he placed his lips on Allison's.

And throughout Kris' stay, every now and then they would slip away to this haven to quietly enjoy each other's presence.

Chapter 8

It was the Saturday after the fourth of July at the breakfast table when Eleanor broke down and cried. Fred had been gone now for five weeks, and she couldn't get over the fact that he was no longer sitting at the breakfast table. Fred had built the house thirty years earlier when they were married, and for those thirty years Fred had always sat opposite Eleanor at the table. The breaking of the thirty-year tradition was, at times, just more than she could take. But it was more than eating together, and sleeping together, and the little things. Sometimes it was just missing the fact that they got into each other's way.

And while Allison and Kris talked to Eleanor, their words were empty, for this was something that Eleanor could only work out for herself. No one else could help her. For some time to come, the good days and the bad, would interweave with each other in Eleanor's heart and mind.

Late that same morning Allison, Todd and Kris decided to walk to town for an ice cream cone and to also pick up a few things from the store. As they walked along the sidewalk of the small business section, Todd saw one of his friends from school on the other side of the street who had just returned from a summer sports camp. Telling Allison and Kris where he was going, Todd darted across the street without looking and ran out in front of a car coming up the street. The car struck Todd and he passed beneath the vehicle being rolled and tumbled along the road as the car moved over him, before it could stop. The car stopped about twenty feet past the point where Todd lay in the road.

Todd lay on his back, his left leg broken and contorted beneath his right leg, his right hand lay across his chest, bleeding, with a large portion of the skin scraped away. His left hand lay at his side with two fingers broken and a large bleeding gash across the back of his hand. Blood oozed from his nostrils and the corners of his mouth.

Kris and Allison ran to Todd. Allison screamed as she looked at her brother's body lying dead on the street. She buried her face into Kris' chest and cried aloud. Kris stood holding Allison in his arms, his eyes looking skyward away from Todd, ignoring the *appearance* of what he saw. A crowd gathered quickly and the lady who was driving the car stood nearby, weeping.

Allison tried to stop crying, biting her lower lip. "Why?" she cried, "Why? Oh God, why? This is going to kill my mother. First Daddy, now Todd. Dear God, why? . . . Todd, you fool, why didn't you look where you were going." Kris squeezed her tighter, bringing his right hand to the back of her head as it lay on his shoulder.

After several minutes Dr. Moser came running from

his office down the block. He knelt beside Todd, checking his eye dilation and pulse. Standing up, he removed
his white smock and laid it across Todd's chest and face.
He stepped to Allison and touched her on the arm.
"Allison, I'm sorry, but Todd is gone."

Allison cried even harder, squeezing her hands into
fists, her fingernails penetrating the skin on the palms of
her hands.

Looking him square in the eye Kris spoke calmly and
softly, "Dr. Moser, remove your coat from Todd . . .
you're going to suffocate him."

"What!" Dr. Moser exclaimed in a hushed voice.

Kris released Allison and moved closer to Dr. Moser,
"I said remove your coat or you will suffocate Todd."

Talking through gritted teeth in a quiet but angry
voice, Dr. Moser said, "Listen young man, the boy has
suffered massive internal injuries. He is dead. Don't make
it any harder on Allison by this kind of talk."

Kneeling down, Kris gently removed the coat from
Todd's body and held it in both hands by the collar so
that Dr. Moser could put it back on. Furious, Dr. Moser
snatched the coat away from Kris and looked at him with
eyes full of hate.

With a crowd of at least sixty people gathered
around, Kris stood looking down at Todd's body. In a
voice that was spoken with calm authority and sternness,
but yet so full of love, Kris spoke once, and only once
the words, "Todd, get up."

The broken fingers on Todd's left hand jerked, his leg
straightened, then a small gasp for air from his mouth,
then a larger one, then a tremendous inhalation of air
which raised his chest high, then he exhaled. Todd
opened his eyes and looked around momentarily, then
slowly rose to his feet. Never before in history has a

crowd stood so quietly, so unbelieving of what they were seeing.

Kris removed a handkerchief from his pocket and walked to a lady who was standing in the crowd holding a paper cup filled with coke and ice. He reached his hand into the cup and removed a clump of ice and wrapped it in his handkerchief. Returning to Todd he began to wipe the blood from Todd's face, his arms and hands. As the wet cloth passed over Todd's cuts and scrapes the blood was washed away, cuts healed and the missing skin replaced, not leaving even the slightest indication anywhere on Todd's body that an accident had occurred.

Todd stood with a slight smile on his face and a never seen before twinkle in his eyes as he looked at Kris. Raising his right hand to Todd's shoulder, Kris smiled and spoke, "I hope you've learned to watch where you are going. Your mother isn't going to be too happy to hear about her fourteen year old boy doing something dumb like this."

Three o'clock that afternoon found Kris sitting in the shade of one of the weeping willow trees in front of the house. Allison hadn't spoken a word to Kris since the accident. She, like everyone else who saw the accident, was baffled by what had happened. In her heart and soul she knew what had happened, but her conscious mind refused to believe it. In a way, she was almost frightened of Kris, yet filled with awe and love.

The only thing explained to Eleanor was that Todd had been careless by running in front of a car, was hit but not hurt. The stories spreading across town would soon take care of telling the whole tale. Eleanor was upset with Todd for his foolishness and grounded him for a week, confined to the house and yard.

Todd came out of the house, down the front walk

and sat next to Kris under the tree. Looking at him, Todd said, "Kris, *I know who you are.* I saw who you were today uptown when I was hit by the car."

Kris just looked at Todd with a smile in his eyes and nodded, then picked a stubble of weed and stuck it between his teeth.

"Kris, a few seconds after I was hit by the car today . . . Well, I knew that I was dead, at least my body was dead. And as much, and as badly as I wanted to come back to this earth and into my body, I couldn't. You, and what you are, were the key to my coming back, and you brought me back exactly as I had left, in perfect health. I mean, what can I say to you? How do I thank you?"

Kris pulled the weed from his mouth and rolled it around between his thumb and forefinger. "You already have, Todd."

Folding his legs as he sat, Todd brought his elbows to rest on his slightly raised knees. "You know you've changed my whole life, don't you? Those five minutes changed my entire life. Nothing will ever be the same again. It's like I went from a little boy to a . . . to, I don't know what. It's more than a man . . . it's . . . I just can't explain it. I just see everything so differently now . . . you know, for what it really is.

"And that feeling when you told me to get up. It was like my physical body became a vacuum cleaner and just sucked me back into it. I was over across the street watching what was going on with some people I used to know. When you spoke those words I could see my body straighten out . . . you know, my broken bones heal, and all that. I was drawn closer and closer, and the next thing I remember I was standing there looking at you."

Kris continued to listen but showed no signs of

emotion. He just sat there with that piece of weed in his lips looking straight ahead.

Todd paused for a moment, then continued. "You know I saw my dad today, and by grandparents, and a lot of other people I used to know. I even saw Peter Edmonds. He died when he was in the first grade with me. They were all there waiting for me, helping me to make that big step from this world to theirs. They all seemed so full of love and caring.

"Then . . . well, I also saw my mother down here and knew who she was and why I had been born to her, and why Allison is my sister. I also saw all the dumb and foolish things that I've done and how I've hurt other people. I've *really* learned. I'll sure think twice before I ever do anything again . . . I mean anything."

Kris interrupted, still looking straight ahead as he spoke, "Don't ever forget that, Todd. Never. You are a fortunate person. Don't ever lose what you were able to learn today. There is only one sin that people can commit while they are on this earth, and that is *to do something that you know is not right*. That's all there is. You learned that today. You were able to see where you have been wrong. What you did wrong before was not a sin because you didn't know any better. It's only when you know better and go ahead and do it anyway that it counts against you. Just because you didn't know any better when you did something doesn't make it right, either. *You'll have to correct all your wrongs in time unless you learn from them now.*"

"Yes," Todd replied, "I see that so very clearly now."

Todd reached down and picked at the grass with his fingers. "You know, Kris, when I saw you today, it was just hard for me to believe, yet it didn't surprise me any, either. And like I said before, I know why I am here with

Allison . . . and I also know why you are here with her."
Todd paused, picked up a piece of grass examining it very
closely, then continued, "You really love her, don't
you?"

Kris nodded his head, "Can't ever remember her not
being there . . . in my heart, or in my soul," he said as
tears formed in his eyes.

"When I saw you today, Kris, it was almost as if there
was some type of link between you and Allison, almost
like a rope tying you two together. And . . . well . . . I
also know that you're going to be leaving soon, especially
after today . . . ."

"What else did you see today, Todd?" Kris asked as
he moved his head, wiping the tears from the corners of
his eyes on his shirt sleeve.

"Well, I saw who my wife is going to be."

"You mean Sally McPherson?"

"Yes, how did you know?" Todd said, then continued in an apologetic voice, "guess I don't need to ask
that question do I? It's kind of hard to believe that that
skinny, little ten year old girl will someday be my wife.
Kris, is that really true?"

"Yes, But what is more surprising, is who would have
been your wife if today had not happened."

"What do you mean?"

"Well, Sally is quite an enlightened little girl, and
now, today, you are quite an enlightened young man. But
if today had not happened you would have continued as
you were going and would have selected another of your
soul mates as your wife. Who that girl would have been is
not important any longer."

"I see . . . well, at least I think I do," Todd said. "It's
just all so unreal. It's like I am living life at a completely
different level."

"You are," Kris said as he turned and faced Todd, "but don't ever let that go to your head. It will be easy now for you to understand in your mind the rights and wrongs of a situation, but you will find it very difficult to understand these things in your heart, to carry them through into all your actions and deeds. That is the real test, to live what you understand life to be.

"For instance, you can see as a result of today that what you hear in the church that you go to is not completely correct. But don't be a rebel and stop going, or condemn them for what they believe. Just try and understand them and learn from them. When the time is right for you to leave, you will know it.

"You see, Todd, that is a problem in today's world, people see something new and they rebel against the old and a conflict results. *The only way to convince people of anything is to set an example.* If you believe in love, then be loving and people will see it. And in love, you love everyone and everything. If there is one person you cannot love, or one creature whose welfare you cannot care about, then you don't yet understand love. And if you want peace, live peace and people will see it. You can't rebel, protest, riot, and kill your way into a peaceful society. Be a perfect example, *be a perfect demonstration of what you believe in.* And sometimes that may hurt, and sometimes it may crush you to stand up for what you believe, sometimes you may feel as though you are dying inside, and sometimes it may seem easier to just give up. But if that is what you believe in, then you must hold to it regardless of the cost. And there will be those who will rob you of everything you have to give, and those who will take away from you everything that you have ever cared about, but you can't give up. For if you do, then you never really believed it, and it was only a passing trend.

"And at times when you know that something is true and right, there may be situations and appearances that portray just the opposite. And these will be the times that test your beliefs, that will test your heart . . . that will test your heart and your very soul.

"Just remember, you cannot shove anything down someone's throat and expect them to believe it. The only way you learn in school is by working the problems, to put into practice the theory you have learned. And if you don't believe in something, then don't try and pretend that you do, because people will see through you like you were a piece of glass.

"Todd, believe in love and peace, believe in caring and giving, believe in God, so when someone looks at you they will know beyond any doubt that they all exist, and that they are all obtainable."

Chapter 9

It was Sunday morning after church and the minister had invited the congregation to stay and review some literature that had been assembled in the classrooms as part of a religion cultural exchange program. Allison browsed by the tables of books and pamphlets. Her eyes scanned across one of the tables, then stopped as one book seemed as if it had leaped off the table to get her attention. It was from India and entitled KRSNA: THE HIGHEST INDIVIDUALIZATION OF LOVE IN MAN. She picked it up, walked to a chair and began looking through it.

The Haynes' were still at church as Kris sat on the front porch swing. He heard a car pull up to the curb and stop. When he looked to see who it was, it didn't surprise him that it was the town sheriff. As the sheriff got out of the car Kris could see that he was in his early fifties, of a small, thin build, graying hair, and wearing silver rimmed glasses. As he came up the walk towards Kris he adjusted the holster on his hip, then reached up and tugged at the knot of his tie. Stepping onto the porch the sheriff said, "Good morning young man, are you Kris?"

Standing up and shaking hands, Kris replied, "Yes . . . I'm Kris McDaniels. Can I help you?"

"Kris, I'm Sheriff Aycock. I, ah . . . I want to talk to you about what happened yesterday up in town. Dr. Moser seemed to be pretty upset. He's been pretty dumfounded by what happened to little Amy Patterson . . . and then . . . ah, yesterday. Let me tell you son, you've got Dr. Moser a little frightened because he can't explain all of this."

The sheriff's voice got a little more stern as he raised his right foot to the seat of a chair, bent over and rested his arm on his leg. "In fact, you've got quite a bit of this town frightened. There's all kinds of talk and rumors going on about you. Let me ask you something, son, who are you and why'd you come here his summer?"

Kris tried to explain what he could, but it was of no use, the sheriff's mind was fixed. He tried to explain that he hadn't hurt anyone, that he only cared about people, that he was only trying to help those that he could. But the sheriff's ears couldn't hear Kris' words. After quite a lengthy, one-sided, discussion, Sheriff Aycock looked down at Kris and said in a sour and bitter voice, "Son, I suggest you give some serious thought to leaving if you really don't have any business here in town."

Allison was the last person to leave the church. Eleanor and Todd had been sitting in the car waiting for quite some time. Allison seemed to have a renewed spirit about her as they rode home, and she was finally wanting to talk with Kris. It had been almost twenty-four hours since she had spoken to him.

Eleanor worked in the kitchen preparing lunch while

Allison and Kris sat out on the front porch talking. Allison had apologized for not speaking but tried to explain some of the thoughts of fear and wonderment that had been going through her mind. After a few minutes pause she took a deep breath, then said, "I saw a book at church today. It was called KRSNA. Are you familiar with that book?"

"Oh I've heard of it and know a little bit about it, I suppose. I've never really read it though."

"Kris, is that where your name comes from? The spelling is just about the same, except you have an 'I' in your name."

"I believe that's it."

"Krsna is supposed to be a very special person according to the book. He is supposed to be full of love and possess some very special powers. Is that what happened to Amy and Todd . . . I mean, are you Krsna?"

"No . . . yes . . . maybe . . . I'm just me. Krsnas exist on this earth by the tens of thousands. Allison, the only difference between them and me is that this time I was not born to this earth. I just appeared here six weeks ago. It's happened before . . . sometimes exceptions are made and people don't necessarily have to be born. It doesn't happen often, but it does happen. I don't believe I will ever have the opportunity to do this again. But I had to take the one chance I had and spend it with you. And while I am here I am hopefully helping the people that I wanted to, and any others that happen to come my way."

Allison sat listening, not really knowing what to say.

"You see, Allison, the only difference between me and the other Krsnas is that they are born to this earth and grow up accumulating all the race consciousness along the way. *The limitations we place on ourselves can be very powerful* . . . extremely powerful. These false appearances are the things that we need to overcome.

"I possess no special powers that you don't have. The only difference is that I have discovered them, and as yet, you haven't. But you will. The fact that you now know they exist will help you to discover them. We have all been blessed with the power and ability to control our lives. Some choose to use the power themselves, while others let someone else's power control their life, then continually ask why things are going so badly for them.

"One thing you must remember is that I am absolutely no different than you in my so-called powers and abilities. *The level to which you understand anything governs your ability to use it effectively.* The more you understand it, the better you can use it. And that is true of mathematics, electricity, driving a car, or using the power of your mind. And in the end, it all boils back down to love. For when you love everything, without exception or prejudice, then everything will respond to your words and to your thoughts, as long as they are given in love. For *love only knows love.*"

They continued their conversation for quite some time, Kris trying to explain what things in life are real and those which are false. He tried to explain that the only real thing in the universe is love, and anything that is contrary to love is created out of man's inability to see things unselfishly. He told her that if you could not find love, or God, in your fellowman you would never discover Him any other place.

He tried to explain that everything is made from intelligent substance, that the hardest steel and stones of granite are created from atoms that are vibrantly alive, which function according to laws of intelligence. "And where there is intelligence," he summarized, "there is love. And everything, without exception, must respond to love."

Looking into Allison's beautiful eyes, Kris continued, "And that is why I am here, Allison, because of my love for you. And while I love you this minute as a man, and I love you more than any man has ever loved before, it is nothing compared to what lives in my soul for you. And while I love you, there are also others here who love you, one of whom you will meet soon.

"We have lived on this earth many, many times together. We have walked together as brothers and sisters, friends, and as a husband and wife. Then in one lifetime I finished all my lessons and I no longer had to come back, but I still do for various reasons.

"Allison . . . you have been interwoven into my soul for the rest of eternity. And here on this earth you are the air I breathe, the beat of my heart, the blood in my veins, you are my every thought, my every dream, my every prayer. You are the sunrise and sunset, you are the moon, the stars, and the sky. Allison, you have been every answer to all answers I have found.

"And Allison, it is such a wonderful and fulfilling thought, to think that some day every soul will experience within the spirit of its being, comparable feelings that I have for you."

Chapter 10

Crank calls and anonymous letters were worse than ever on Monday. And those that searched for short-cuts to the truth and those that sincerely sought, filled the front yard again. Pressure was growing on Eleanor, in fact on the entire household, for privacy was almost impossible at times. In a private moment with Eleanor, Kris apologized for the inconveniece but explained that he would be leaving very soon, very soon. He asked that she not mention it to Allison since they had agreed not to discuss it anymore.

And that same night the monthly Town Council Meeting discussed only Kris McDaniels, who he could be, where he came from, and what business he had being in town.

Tuesday morning at five-thirty Kris slipped out of his bedroom window onto the ledge and climbed up to the highest spot on the roof. He sat there, legs tucked into his chest, arms wrapped around his legs, chin resting on his knees awaiting the pending sunrise.

The sky slowly grew red, orange, purple, and pink in color, each displayed in its own perfect pattern as the sun came closer to the horizon. As it peeked into view tears ran from Kris' eyes. How many sunrises had he seen? A hundred thousand, a million, a billion? Yet the awe, the beauty, the wonderment never ceased to fill him, never stopped speaking the message that today was a new day, a day that exists so that we may start to live again, a day to learn, a day to correct the mistakes of our past, another day that has been given to us out of love, a love that is beyond human understanding.

Todd was confined to the house, but Allison and Kris continued their tradition and walked to the drug store during the late morning for an ice cream cone. As they approached the drug store they could see that scaffolds had been erected in front of the store since it was to be remodeled on the outside. They stopped and watched as a forklift lowered two tons of new bricks on one of the scaffolds. The work crew broke for lunch, then Allison and Kris went inside.

As they sat there eating their cones, an old high school girl friend of Allison's came in and they began to talk. After a few minutes Kris interrupted and said that he was going outside to look at what was planned for the store. Squeezing Allison's hand and winking at her, he turned around on the swivel stool, got up, and walked outside.

No one was nearby as Kris walked beneath the scaffold containing the bricks overhead. Without any apparent human cause, it collapsed, and two tons of orange and red colored bricks crushed Kris McDaniels against the sidewalk as they fell.

Sheriff Aycock and Dr. Moser stood and watched as the workmen removed the bricks. Allison looked on, tears pouring heavily from her eyes, yet she made no noise, not even a whimper.

Dr. Moser stood up shaking his head, saying softly, "He's dead."

Sheriff Aycock removed the wallet from Kris' rear pocket and opened it. It was completely empty, no drivers license or money, except for an envelope that had been folded over three times and was stuck in the paper money compartment. He removed the envelope and unfolded it. On the outside was written:

My name is Krisna James McDaniels. I have no parents or relatives. In the event of my death please have me cremated as soon as possible. I wish no ceremony or grave. Please scatter my ashes to the wind that it may take them where it pleases. Money to cover the cost of cremation is inside.

Opening the envelope Sheriff Aycock found six new twenty dollar bills.

When Allison returned to the house, Kris' room was completely empty of clothes and all of his belongings. Eleanor and Todd insisted that no one had been inside the house all morning but them.

Chapter 11

It was five o'clock that afternoon and Allison lay on the porch swing asleep. Winds out of the east were already carrying Kris' ashes across the green countryside, the pasture down by the river, and the blueberry patches now full of ripe berries. And somewhere in eastern Ohio, Marjorie Preston finished reading her first book.

As she slept, Kris came to Allison in the form of a dream. They lay in the pasture on a checkered blanket near the river, sun shining extra bright overhead. Kris lay propped up on his right elbow looking with that special look, deep into Allison's eyes. "I'm sorry I had to leave this way," he said, "but I promised we would never discuss it again, and I could not tell you how I would leave. I had to do it this way, because if I had just disappeared you would have always been waiting for me to return.

"This is not a dream, Allison, it is really me talking to you. You see, there is really no such thing as death. I just wanted to remind you that I've always been with you, and

I always will be. You will be meeting someone who will become very special to you within a year or so and I want you to know that I will be right here to help you when, and where I can.

"I will always help you, Allison, but there is a law that we must both adhere to: *I cannot help unless you ask me to.* So please never hesitate to ask me. You will never be able to ask too many times, or ask too much. When you ask, just relax and try to let the answer come. It will be felt, seen, or heard through the voice of your intuition.

"Allison, I must leave now, but first let me thank you . . . thank you so very much for the summer. And I want to tell you this, just one last time. I love you . . . I do love you so very much," Kris said, then pressed his lips upon Allison's.

She awoke quickly, startled by Kris' conversation, and his kiss that seemed more real than when he was here on earth. Allison sat up on the swing, and as she did so Amy came up the sidewalk and turned onto the front walk leading to the porch.

Amy wore her yellow dress from that Saturday many weeks before, only this time she wore matching yellow knee socks.

Halfway up the walk she stopped, closed her eyes, and outstretched her arms. Her lips could be seen moving slightly. And from over the house top came a dozen or so bluebirds which circled around her head, then began landing on her arms, shoulders, hands . . . .